July, 2016

For Hampton Library,
my personal favorite ——
A joyful OY! with love
from Monte; Me ——

♡ Danielle
Lavery ——

MONTE
&
THE MONTE VISTA HOTEL

The Hampton Library in Bridgehampton
P.O. Box 3025
Bridgehampton, NY 11932

MONTE AND THE MONTE VISTA HOTEL
The love story of one cat, one hotel:
rescue and reclamation

Danielle Lavery

The Hampton Library in Bridgehampton
P.O. Box 3025
Bridgehampton, NY 11932

Dedicated to those who are found
and to those who do the finding.

Contents

Hello, Everybody,

I am Monte. The Monte Vista is my hotel. Well, if you must know, Sue and Barney actually own the hotel. Nevertheless, they give me free reign, and as we all know—cats rule!

Oh, the stories I could tell...

Will tell.

Starting here. Starting now.

First off, my credo:

"All things are possible in the feline universe."

Powerful?

It works for me.

Extraordinary good fortune linked me to Sue and Barney. Was it love at first sight for Sue, Barney, and me? You might ask them. For my part, it was Hallelujah! Jubilation!

Located in historic Black Mountain, North Carolina, the three-story hotel was in foreclosure, dilapidating moment to moment, frozen pipes and all. I lived here hungry and emaciated, in a cellar fraught with peril, deep in the murky shadows of the vast, dark, scary basement of an unoccupied hotel.

Good thing I was born to be brave. In order to survive I developed my hunting skills: infinite patience, an accurate pounce, and a terrific sense of timing. My creds as a huntress are well-established. But more about that, later.

You might say that I came with the property as an unexpected bonus when Sue and Barney decided to buy the hotel and restore it to its former glory.

Does that make me a foundling?

An abandoned stray, I am blessed with good looks and a selectively engaging personality. I am a lady-cat, and that's that.

Everyone calls me Monte. My full name is
Monte Vista. I am so totally named after
the hotel. How original is that? But, I tell
you, when Sue summons me with "Monte
Vista!" and there is a lilt in her voice, I
know that she is in a very good mood, and
there is a treat in store for me. Monte Vista
is the hotel and Monte Vista is me.
I am glad to be me.

Celebrity?

I hasten to add that because I am beautiful
and often affectionate, I am quite popular
with the hotel staff and guests. I warn you,
though, I am known to ignore and to evade
those who chase after me, calling, "Here,
kitty-kitty." Really!

I am a dainty cat. The only time you will see me dash is when some kind soul opens the front door for me. Actually, I bolt!

My walk is purposeful. I do not lollygag, unless of course, I am investigating or on surveillance. Truly, I can be affectionate.

You will know that you have found favor with me if I sidle over to you and weave in and out between your ankles with my tail fully extended. I might even hop onto your lap and knead your thighs, or I might just sit on your lap, in full purr. And this, of course, is contingent on your being a "cat person," an ailurophile, as it were.

Pedigree

How does an abandoned kitten claim
heritage?

Let me count the ways.

American born, I am of indeterminate
lineage. Parentage? Hopefully not too
indiscriminant. Nonetheless, I am
deemed to be of Random-Breed. My
coloring is Russian Blue, offset by
tuxedo markings. My eyes vary from
green to amber.

My dainty demeanor belies the feral
nature of my hugely successful hunting
prowess.

Bottom line?

I am an American beauty.

Finn

Madison

FRIENDS AND FAMILY

Living in an action-packed hotel brings many wonderful people and unique relationships into my life. Here are two of my favorites.

Finn

From time to time, one little boy named Finn brings his parents to dine at the Monte Vista. His father comes for the steak. His mother comes for the vegetable lasagna. Finn? He's here for the great burger, the maraschino cherries, and me! After he very slowly savors each of three cherries, he approaches me with sticky fingers.

Initially, he lunged for me, and I had to leap from his clutches!

Now, however, he is most gentle with me, and we have become friends. He carefully pets me. We talk. We snuggle. We laugh. We giggle. We bond. I purr loudly for awhile, and then I am on my way.

He's happy.

I'm happy.

Everybody's happy!

Madison

Truly, I am most happy when Sue and Barney's granddaughter, Madison, comes for a holiday with her mom, Christine. Every few months, they reluctantly leave all of their many animals at home in Colorado to come see us at the hotel.

We think Madison is an animal whisperer. Certainly she intuits and lights up my world.

Last visit, the two of us painted a small table for the lobby. What fun! My contribution was to indicate colors. It was a real collaboration, I tell you.

We expect Madison to become a veterinarian, which will bode well for me, especially in my old age.

SO: BACK TO THE HUNT

We are critter-free at the Monte Vista Hotel.

Thanks to me, critters think twice before they tarry at the Monte Vista. My reputation as an avid huntress remains intact.

Seriously, I am a lady-cat. And that's that.

Except.

Except when I am hunting, all bets are off.

For I am a huntress *extraordinaire*.

Since the cellar critters are gone, I am left to venture outdoors in pursuit of the hunt. I view it as my part of the neighborhood watch.

I continue to hunt on a daily basis, and I know where the hunting is good.

This, my small-game safari, is my time of mystery. Although eventually there are tales of "sightings," nobody knows where I go or how far I venture off the property. (Far.)

It is my time to gallivant, to explore the boundaries of the neighborhood—even the "hollers" nearby. The hollers are wooded ravines that house families of bears and coyotes.

Personally, I skirt the hollers out of respect for these inhabitants. They are rarely encountered, but they do live here.

For my part, there is no need for us to meet.

One great feature of this mountainous area of Western North Carolina is that humans and animals co-exist with something akin to an abiding respect for one another. Traffic will stop for any bear crossing Highway 70 in front of the hotel, after which the bear unaccountably disappears...

Barney and Sue prefer that I practice "catch-and-release" when I hunt. I much prefer to bring my prey home, to get through the front door. Barney and Sue will interrupt whatever they're doing to intercept me and divest me of my prey.

I tell you, I keep them agile.

THE INCIDENT

Friday nights are full tilt at the Monte Vista Hotel, particularly in summer, when the patios are open.

I confess, I did cause patio pandemonium one beautiful summer evening.

The First Friday art opening and reception had just concluded, so the lobby was still filled with guests. The dining room hosted a large wedding rehearsal dinner. A private dinner party prevailed on the side porch. The cocktail lounge was standing-room-only, as people clamored for the bartenders' attention. The patio had not one empty table as the outdoor musicians began to play. The overflowing parking lots should have tipped me off...

But no.

THIS is when I returned vainglorious from the hunt! Totally oblivious, I pranced up the front steps and hurtled through the open front door, carrying my prey—a small rabbit—in my mouth.

What was I thinking?

Clearly, no thinking was involved.

The lobby went into an uproar! The bar and outdoor cocktail area went into an uproar! Pandemonium erupted outside as I careened across the patio bricks, with Sue in hot pursuit!

Shrieks ricocheted through the patio. Chairs scraped across the bricks, some overturned, as dinner guests jumped up from their seats to try to separate me from my rabbit.

Sue cut a swath among the tables and swept me up on the far side of the patio as I let go of the rabbit. She held me close and assuaged my terror as we strode inside.

How fortunate am I that Sue fully realizes and appreciates my dual nature of feral huntress and affectionate feline. She loves me as I am. In for a penny, in for a pound...

Unconditional love. That's us.

FAUNA... THE GARDEN... MY DREAM...

Really, the only fauna you are likely to find outdoors at the hotel consist of bumble bees, butterflies, dragonflies, ladybugs, and the occasional rabbit or squirrel. Sue's gardens are purged of voles, thanks to me.

The gardens include a mint patch. Which brings me to my dream. Do cats dream?

This one does.

When Sue goes out to her mint garden, I follow, and I dream that ONE day, I will have my own catnip garden!

Sue is good at intuiting my preferences and needs. Will she be able to intuit my dream? Can we take it to the next level?

Monte to Sue...   Monte to Sue...

TRANSFORMATION:
THE HOTEL GETS A FACE-LIFT

The Monte Vista Hotel is buff, now.

How did Barney, Sue, and I transform a dump into a palace?

Sue and Barney did it, much of it themselves, with their friend and foreman, Rick. Naturally, I oversaw the proceedings.

Imagine! Months and months of demolition, reconstruction, floor sanding, skill saws, jack hammers. ... The noise! The mess! The frenzy!

The glory of it!

First off, in the lobby, the disintegrating portieres were dragged down from the windows, unleashing a dust storm of major proportions (cough, cough). Decades of Monte Vista history were unfurled and released. Scattered were endless memory motes: the lazy summer afternoons with the ladies fanning themselves at bridge parties, the tea sandwiches, the sweet tea, the weddings, the receptions.

Today, the lobby is a sparkling realm with unadorned windows. The window sills feature beautiful vases, sculptures, and orchids.

Early days, curious as I was, I stayed out of the way. Nevertheless, I did help Sue with the design and redesign, to outfit the lobby and 46 guest bedrooms. We trekked our footprints to and fro through the construction dust, as Sue carried bolts of fabric, paint swatches, bedspreads, curtains, and carpet samples.

Here I will tell you about the day I innocently left my paw prints on the newly varnished lobby floor. What a calamity. Barney had closed off the entrances and exits to the lobby. However, the door to the cellar was open. I entered the lobby from the basement, walked over to the central staircase, and thus left my paw prints on the wet floor.

Sue was the first one to see the trail of my dried prints, and she quickly asked foreman Rick if anything could be done to eradicate them. Alas, no way, said Rick. The area would have to be refinished.

Oh, boy.

Now this is what I want you to know.
Barney, exhausted as he was after all
that work, was not angry with me. And
that was when I again realized that I
am loved... truly loved.

Beyond wood floor restoration, the
transformation included walls and
woodwork painted. New fire escapes.
New tiles laid in the large kitchen. New
heating and air-conditioning systems
installed. New lighting. New tables
made for the dining room, along with a
new wall unit for the lobby. All new
carpeting for the staircases.

The creation of a brand-new bar. Newly
bricked rear and side patios.
Installation of a new stone floor for
front porch and steps. Trees pruned.
Barney even lined the driveway with
new carriage lamps.

A new green awning over the front entrance capped it all perfectly.

The installing of a new roof was particularly exciting for me, being three stories up with a steep pitch. Naturally, I climbed the ladders and walked the periphery to inspect the workmanship, up close and personal. I traversed the entire length of the roof. Lithe creature that I am, I gingerly descended by the same ladders, head first. Barney saw me and dropped what he was doing, to act as my spotter.

Not so easy, I tell you.

Today, The Monte Vista Hotel is buff, indeed.

Reclaimed.

My home, the Monte Vista Hotel.

PITCHING WOO...
DALLIANCES

I have had my share of dalliances, some great, some not so great. Sue was surprised, early on, when she took me to the vet to be spayed. She was amazed to learn that I had already had the surgery. No progeny from me. Sad, actually.

Blackie

Prior to Sue and Barney's arrival at the hotel, I occasionally shared the hotel with a vagabond cat named Blackie. Young love's dream? I thought so. For awhile there, Blackie hung the moon...

But no.

For me, Blackie was a cautionary tale.

Huge folly on my part. Beware flash, dash, and brash!

Some might deem him a blackguard. He is easily recognized because he is missing half of his tail. (Ask me no questions.)

Blackie was an early suitor in my survival days. Alas, he proved to be a selfish, dastardly cad—at the very least, an insensitive oaf.

Admittedly, after Sue and Barney arrived and befriended me, I became territorial with regard to sharing the hotel with Blackie. Besides, Blackie would appropriate my food.

The day came when I stood my ground.

What began as a territorial tangle exploded into molten fury—a fierce, no-holds-barred caterwaul of epic proportions. The fur flew!

"OUCH! Ouch, Ouch, Ouch, Ouch, Ouch."

Sue, the solitary witness, had to break us up with a broom. Thank goodness it was early days in the hotel construction, and the hotel had not yet opened.

Fortunately, I was not disfigured. I bear no scars, physically.

That was the end of it. Blackie is off my radar. No loss and no misgivings whatsoever on my part.

As *felis non grata,* he no longer frequents the hotel, although Sue will occasionally see him peering down on us from high atop the breezeway roof.

Malibu

Briefly, Malibu, a neighborhood newcomer, paid court. He was acclimating after a move from Atlanta, where he was strictly an indoor cat.

His family had moved into a fairy tale cottage across the street.

Picture this: Malibu is gorgeous, a white cat with ginger markings. Bigger than I am, he is winsome, and he is well-groomed, a real plus in my book.

But here's the thing. When Malibu paid me a visit, we sat atop the front steps to the hotel, one to each side. We traded hunting tips, for, amazingly, he is a born hunter.

And that's it.

Sue thought we resembled Fu dogs or lions, protecting the front portal to the hotel.

Malibu is gorgeous but ho-hum to the nth degree.

A real nonstarter. That train never left the station. Sigh...

I tell you, when it comes to pitching woo, Malibu could bore for North Carolina.

In any event, Malibu is a moot point now, his family having moved across town.

Do I dally now?

...Not on property.

A CHANGE OF MENU

Now that I am "rescued," my menu and food preferences have changed. Previously, small critters comprised my diet. Nowadays, Barney and Sue notice and indulge my food preferences. As a beloved hotel resident, I have come to enjoy certain prepared cat foods. Chicken with cheese is a favorite.

Fish? Not so much. Nothing with fish, actually, if you don't mind.

Snacks? I occasionally indulge. Dairy products are my favorite. Give me a bit of cheese and I am happy. Ice cream blisses me out.

A highlight of my day is my predawn breakfast with Sue, who gives me a saucer of cream. This is our quiet, private time, quite special to me.

My main meal of the day is served at 4 p.m.—my feline version of "high tea."

Talk about feline aesthetics.

DAILY ROUTINE

I am pretty much omnipresent at the hotel, but I do have my getaways.

My days are generally configured like this:

5 a.m.—Breakfast with Sue, before daybreak, followed by my walkabout outside.

6:30 a.m.—Sue and I call her mother in Florida for a good, long chat.

7-10 a.m.—Continental breakfast brings guests downstairs.

11 a.m.—Checkout! You will usually find me lazing in the shafts of sunbeams slanting into the lobby. I like to stretch full out on the sun-warmed hardwood floors, mid-lobby.

This way, I get to observe guest checkouts. Do give me a wave in farewell from across the room as you depart the hotel!

Midmorning, chances are that I will head out to hunt. (Unless it rains. Rain distresses me, big time, and keeps me indoors.) In early afternoon, I help welcome the new guests at check-in.

Afternoons, post hunt and post my "high tea," are for napping outside in the sun or on the front porch.

Come twilight, it's cocktail hour in the bar, the lobby, or perhaps outside on the patio.

Mingle, mingle, mingle, that's me!

Evenings are spent on walkabouts in the hotel or contentedly bonding with Barney at the front desk until bedtime.

Often our evening snack is ice cream. Yum.

You might wonder where I sleep. Decidedly not in one of the 46 beautifully restored guest rooms. Originally at night, I served as silent sentinel, usually on a carpeted stair landing in front of a warm radiator. I must admit, though, that I prefer to sleep near Sue and Barney.

Occasionally, however, I disappear into the night...

PATIO/FRONT PORCH

On warm sunny days, you will most likely find me on the patio, soaking up the sunshine. As our guests return from sightseeing, mountain hiking, and touring, many will join me to unwind in the dappled sunshine.

Quintessentially restorative.

Another thoroughly enjoyable option is the front porch—cool, shaded with overhead fans whirring as we contemplate the mountains. I am the one in fine feline curlicue form, warmed by the sun.

I am here to absorb the inevitable tall tales and holiday chatter of our guests, and to add a grace note to the Monte Vista Hotel. Goodwill Ambassador, that's me.

Occasionally, however ...

CALCULATING FELINE? ME?

Late one afternoon, I awoke from a dreamy catnap on the front porch to overhear an elderly gentleman talking to his ladywife. As he shook a gnarled, bony finger in my direction, he said, "Felis domestica calculata."

Now I ask you, am I a "calculating feline"?

Hrmph! Persnickety old goat. (Forgive me, here, won't you?)

I will note that although I am not one to readily register feline disdain, I nevertheless launched myself out of there, and with a twitch of my tail, I left them to it.

Really!

The nerve.

INSOUCIANCE

One day, a man and his wife checked into the hotel. Both professors, they were in town for a four-day academic conference. He is memorable because he always wore a beret and a bow tie.

They did not spend much time at the hotel. They paid me no heed. (It happens.)

One morning, I was in the lobby when they sat down with their morning coffees.

"That cat has a certain *je ne sais quoi*," he mused.

Je ne sais quoi? Moi?

"Insouciance," proclaimed his wife.

Insouciance, indeed.

Hrmph!

I unwound from my comfortable curl. I
went into a full stretch. And then I
swung out of there with as much
insouciance as I could muster.

Trust me.

OY!

Although I cannot speak (yet), I love words. I collect them. Do cats do that?

This one does.

"OY!" is my new favorite. It encompasses a wide spectrum of emotion, as I discovered.

One afternoon, as an older man registered at the front desk, he dropped a heavy book on his foot and said, "OY!"

Exclamation of consternation? Hmm.

A day later as he walked through the lobby, he received a telephone call from his daughter—his grandson had passed the state law boards on his first try.

"OY!" the man beamed.

Now it's OY! for joy? What a splendid word.

On the last morning of his stay, en route to his early-morning walk, our guest opened the front door. Pouring rain!

"OY!" he quietly muttered to himself as he closed the door. OY! as disappointment. Wow.

I give you OY! Short and sweet; multifunctional.

I can't say it, but I can think it, and I do.

OLD HOTEL/NEW TRADITIONS

We Support the Arts

There is an old red farmhouse on the property. Sue and Barney have rented it out to an organization of artists for one dollar per year. Thus, "Red House" now houses studio and gallery space for local artists.

The hotel also functions as a sparkling gallery space, promoting local artists via revolving exhibits.

Additionally, as patrons of the arts, Sue and Barney have opened the hotel to a local writers' guild on the third Thursday of every month for networking, readings, and promotion.

On Friday afternoons, the lobby is a gathering place for tatters and knitters who meet to work on projects and to discuss patterns and techniques.

Tatters? Imagine! Tatting, a 200-year-old tradition of making lace, is alive and well at the Monte Vista Hotel.

Annual Garden Party

In early May, the hotel is a harbinger of spring, when the grounds are opened on a Saturday to host the much anticipated town garden show. Gardeners and would-be gardeners gather from miles around to see what's new and beautiful in this year's flora. It's a glorious day of blossoms and seedlings and expert garden advice—a day of box lunches and a day in which Barney revels in the opportunity to operate his hot dog cart.

Chances are that you will not find me at this gorgeous event.

I make an early-morning inspection as the vendors set up their outdoor displays.

I wend my way among the flower pots and the flats of herbs. (Does anybody have catnip this year???)

I venture past the blooming shrubs and trees, past the recycling ladies and their truckload of discarded containers.

And then I retreat to a quiet spot with a good vantage point. (Last year was great. I perched in the middle of a second-floor bridge of the fire escape, which overhangs the side patio.)

So you see, I get to attend, and I do not get trampled.

I tell you, one way or the other, I never miss much at the Monte Vista Hotel.

Christmas Tree Fund-Raiser

From Thanksgiving to New Year's Eve, the lobby, dining room, and porches are aglow with the sparkle and glimmer of 25 trees, each one independently decorated by a local business or organization, as a fund-raiser for a local nonprofit organization. At the base of each tree is a contribution box. Votes are cast by inserting donations into the boxes. The tree with the highest tally wins the competition.

There is actually another category dedicated to my tree preference - "Monte's Fave." Under which tree do I spend the most time soaking up the holiday season? People are actually intrigued by my choice. Go figure.

I must tell you that I am quite proud to be a featured player in this project. The monies raised go into a fund to purchase home heating oil for families in need.

And so it goes—new traditions continue to be created in this wonderful historic hotel.

CAT CAFÉS...
TOKYO ON MY MIND

Bear with me and assume that cats do have a mind.

This one does.

Recently, a woman guest scooped me up off the lobby floor to cuddle and coo. She remarked that our cuddling reminded her of the available cuddles at the cat cafés of Tokyo.

Tokyo? Japan? Cat cafés? It is beyond my ken, but everyone is talking about them. You'll never guess. Cat cafés have gone global in recent years, with Tokyo in the lead with thirty-nine! Whooeee! Go, Tokyo!

Following Tokyo's lead, the first two cat cafés opened in the United States, one in Oakland, California, and the other in New York City, with more to follow. Plans are underway to open one in neighboring Asheville.

The feline universe thus expands, continent to continent.

Hugs and kisses all around...

CATS WHO PAINT

Brace yourself. Sue recently read a book titled *Why Cats Paint.*

Can you imagine?

Me, paint?

So that's our new project—my learning to paint (express myself?) with acrylic paints. (My first work consists of paw prints, but I see the possibilities.) Barney is leery of the mess, but he is a supporter of the arts, and thus, we carry on.

Perhaps when you visit, my very own paintings will be on display!

Who knows?

Maybe even for sale!

RESCUED VS. FOUND: LOVED FOR SURE

I was blessed to be born here. Like Sue and Barney, the people in Black Mountain and the entire Asheville area are well-known for their love of animals and for supporting organizations that promote and facilitate animal rescue and adoption.

Was I rescued? Hmm. You tell me. Technically, I was living on the premises when Sue and Barney arrived. The Monte Vista Hotel was already my domain.

Have they enhanced the quality of my life? Unquestionably.

But rescued? Honestly, I resist being termed a *rescue* cat.

Foundling? Perhaps.

But really, who found whom?

OK. I resonate with foundling—a most fortunate foundling.

"I once was lost, but now am found."

BARNEY, SUE and ME
"en famille"

GRAND FINALE: FAMILY

There you have it. Our love story.

Do cats love?

This one does.

(All things are possible in the feline universe.)

I love you, Sue.

I love you, Barney.

These are halcyon days at the Monte Vista Hotel. With Sue and Barney, I have found the place where I belong. Family.

And it happened right here, at the Monte Vista Hotel.

THE END

Happy is the home with at least one cat.
——Italian proverb

ACKNOWLEDGMENTS

As Monte's scribe, it fell to me to put this book together, only to learn that crafting a book is not for sissies, nor is it a solitary task.

The whole of this book is the sum of its parts. Thanks are due, big time.

With deep gratitude, I salute and embrace those who contributed their talent and support.

Sue Conlon and Barney Fitzpatrick stand first and foremost in so generously opening their hearts to Monte, and their hotel to this venture.

A premier shout-out goes to Maria Cianci, gifted copy-editor and lifelong friend, who nonetheless held my feet to the flame in pursuit of clarity and extraneous commas. (Any grammatical errors are mine alone.)

A joyful OY! to supernovas Daniel Snyder and Walter Somerville for their priceless encouragement.

Along with artists Robyn Gonzalez and Sheila Showers, photographers Gary Leive, Ray Mata, Rick Placke, Carolyn Johnson, Christine Fitzpatrick, Herb Way, and Janey Cope go into my Hall of Fame for bringing beautiful images to Monte's book and social media.

Techno-Wizard Gary Leive parachuted in to navigate the labyrinthian minutiae of the publishing template. As project co-ordinator, he deftly constructed the scaffold of this book, and he did it with grace, mastery, and infinite patience throughout the distillation process. My heartfelt thank you, Gary. Your light illuminates Monte's universe.

Huge thanks to Caroline Fisher and Tony Peele for their patient technical back-up in this work.

Finally, this page serves as a group hug as we envelop Monte, Sue, and Barney in celebration of their story.

D.L.

IMAGE CREDITS

Cover Design: Danielle Lavery, Gary Leive
Cover Photography: Carolyn Johnson

Paw Prints: Gary Leive

With love
to All —
Monte

Sheila H. Showers 2016

AUTHOR

Danielle Lavery, a native New Yorker, resides in Black Mountain, North Carolina, a stone's throw from the Monte Vista Hotel. Also known as Monte's Auntie, she fully supports animal rescue and adoption. This is her first book.

Visit us at:

Monte & The Monte Vista Hotel

@montevistacat

CPSIA information can be obtained at www.ICGtesting.com
Printed in the USA
BVOW06s0617110616

451605BV00001B/2/P